ShowKits

Goldilocks

WHOLE LANGUAGE ACTIVITIES
Patterns for masks, puppets, costumes to use with picture books
by Candy Jones and Lea McGee, illustrated by Marilynn G. Barr

Publisher: Roberta Suid
Editor: Carol Whiteley
Production: Susan Cronin-Paris

ISBN 1-878279-27-0

Printed in the United States of America
9 8 7 6 5 4 3 2 1

For a complete catalog, write to the address above.

Contents

Introduction

Reading folk tales to children introduces them to stories that are an important part of our cultural and literary heritage. ShowKits is designed to help you accompany and extend six traditional folk tales with a variety of drama and movement activities. The activities are appropriate for young children in preschools, kindergartens, child care, after-school programs, and at home.

What Are ShowKits?

Each of the six kits in ShowKits contains materials that focus on helping children explore a well-known and well-loved folk tale: The Three Billy Goats Gruff, The Little Red Hen, The Turnip, Henny Penny, The Three Bears, and The Three Little Pigs.

Each kit provides materials that relate to the folk tale: descriptions of several versions of the folk tale; suggestions for helping children compare two versions of the same folk tale; a movement activity; and reproducible patterns for making props and costumes for the children to use while acting out the story.

Learning with ShowKits

Listening to and learning about folk tales not only encourages understanding of other cultures and ways of life; it can also be the beginning of a child's journey into the world of literature. As children work with the ShowKits materials, comparing different versions of a folk tale, they will gain appreciation of literary styles. As they act out the folk tales or tell them through puppet shows, their language development will be enhanced. The stories' repetitive language appeals to young children and they will enjoy chanting the words during their dramatizations. The movement activities will also provide important development as the children gain gross motor skills and learn language related to body parts and directions.

Getting Ready

The following steps will help you prepare the ShowKits materials for use:

1. Obtain one or more versions of the particular folk tale, using the kit's descriptions of several versions as a guide. The costume and puppet patterns included in each kit were made to fit the first version described—the one marked with an asterisk—but most versions are so similar that you can use almost any version of the story with the patterns.

2. Prepare the LearnTime Chart illustrated in each kit. The chart will help the children learn more about the particular folk tale. Directions for preparing and using each chart are included in the kit.

3. Gather and prepare the materials needed for the PlayTime movement activity. This includes the reproducible pattern provided in most kits.

4. Make the ShowTime props necessary for each kit: spoon puppets, stick puppets, collar costumes, headband and feet costumes, paper plate masks, or body puppets. Each kit provides a list of materials and reproducible patterns plus directions for making and using them. You may want the children to help make the props.

How to Use ShowKits

Begin by reading the folk tale to the children. Then read it again the next day, inviting the children to say aloud the repetitive phrases.

Read the story again the following day. Introduce the show props; you may already have made them, or you may want to have the children help you make them at this point.

Next, select a child to play each character (a list of characters is provided in each kit). Have the children wear the appropriate costumes or hold the particular puppets. If you wish, have all the children sit in a circle and have the appropriate child stand as you read the part of the story that relates to him or her. If you want

the children to stand on a stage, follow the kit's directions on arranging props in a small area much like a stage might be arranged.

Eventually the children may know the story so well that they can act it out or put on a puppet show without you reading the story. Instead you can act as a "side coach," prompting dialogue, or you can be the narrator.

Each day you practice the folk tale show, you may want to include a movement activity. The PlayTime movement activity included in each kit is a natural partner for the dramatic reading and show; it will help release the "wiggles" that come with the excitement of putting on the show.

Once the children become familiar with one version of the folk tale, you may want to use the LearnTime chart activity. This activity will help the children compare different versions of the story, and encourage them to talk about the various authors, characters, action, and vocabulary.

To finish your study of each folk tale, invite the children to retell the story by dictating, drawing, or writing it. The stories the children produce can be collected in a class book to be read along with the other versions of the tale.

The Three Billy Goats Gruff

Story Versions

* <u>The Three Billy Goats Gruff</u> by Ellen Appleby (Scholastic, 1984).

Three billy goats must cross a bridge under which a mean, ugly troll lives. Two goats trick the troll into letting them cross the bridge. The third billy goat butts the troll off the bridge, and all the goats go up the hillside to eat and get fat. (*This version fits the ShowTime patterns included in this kit.)

<u>The Three Billy Goats Gruff</u> by Paul Galdone (Clarion, 1973).

The classic story is illustrated with realistic-looking goats and a fantastic troll.

<u>The Three Billy Goats Gruff</u> by Janet Stevens (Harcourt, 1987).

The first billy goat tricks the troll by dressing in diapers. The second billy goat dresses in a gigantic pair of pants. The third billy goat wears a leather motorcycle jacket and glasses.

Also recommended:

<u>The Three Billy Goats Gruff</u> by Marcia Brown (Harcourt, 1972).

<u>The Three Billy Goats Gruff</u> by Patricia and Fredrick McKissack (Childrens Press, 1987).

<u>The Three Billy Goats Gruff</u> by Tom Roberts (Picture Book Studio, 1989).

<u>The Three Billy Goats Gruff</u> by Jacqueline Smith (Putnam, 1988).

LearnTime Chart Activity

Materials: large sheet of butcher paper, marker, at least two versions of The Three Billy Goats Gruff

Preparation: Make a chart on the butcher paper like the one illustrated here. Hang the chart on a bulletin board or wall.

Activity: Read one version of The Three Billy Goats Gruff aloud. Have the children dictate the information to you to complete the chart. On another day, repeat the process with another version of the story. Compare the two versions. Let the children illustrate the chart by drawing and then cutting out pictures to glue onto it.

	Author	Author
How does the author describe the troll?		
What words does the troll repeat?		
What words do the billy goats repeat?		
What words end the story?		

PlayTime Movement Activity

Materials: brown construction paper, scissors, tape

Preparation: Cut the construction paper into a good number of block-like rectangles. Tape the paper blocks on the floor to form a long bridge.

Activity: Have the children take turns walking along the bridge pretending to be small, middle-sized, and great big billy goats. Then have them tiptoe, jump, skip, gallop, walk backwards, and walk heel-toe along the bridge. Let the children suggest other ways of moving along the bridge.

ShowTime Puppet Show

Characters: Troll; Big, Middle-sized, Small Billy Goats

Materials: ShowTime patterns; box (approx. 20" x 17"); orange, black, white, brown, purple, green, and turquoise felt; small wooden spoon; medium-sized wooden spoon; 2 large wooden spoons; glue; poster board; craft knife; markers; scissors; table

Preparation: Begin by making the spoon puppets. Trace all the billy goat and troll patterns onto the colors of felt indicated. Cut out all the pieces. Glue the felt pieces for the big billy goat to the back of one of the large spoons as indicated. Glue the pieces for the troll to the back of the other large spoon. Glue the pieces for the middle-sized goat to the back of the medium-sized spoon and those for the small goat to the back of the small spoon. See the finished puppets on the first page of this kit.

Next, make the bridge. Fold a large piece of brown felt in half and place the bridge pattern on the fold. Cut, making one complete bridge. Add details as indicated with markers. Cut the box apart as shown and glue on the bridge.

Duplicate the grassy hillside pattern on poster board. Cut the pattern out and add details as indicated with markers. To make the hillside stand alone, cut out two 6" x 3" pieces of poster board. Make a $1\frac{1}{2}$" slit in the center of each piece as shown. Cut two $1\frac{1}{2}$" slits in the grassy hillside and slip the two stands into the slits as shown.

Activity: Set the stage for the puppet show by placing the bridge on a table. Place the hillside to one side. Then let selected children hold the spoon puppets and move them over the bridge as you read or tell the story. Let the children say the repetitive phrases. Repeat the story and the action enough times so that all the children have a chance to participate.

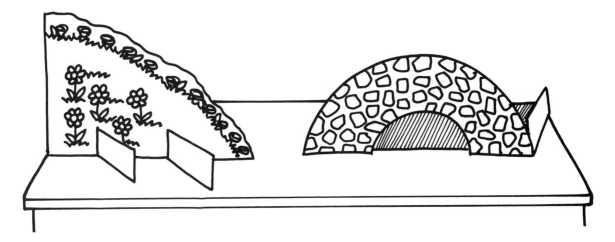

ShowTime Patterns: Troll

hair (purple)

eyebrows (black)

eyes (white)

ears (turquoise)

eyes (black)

mouth (black)

nose (green)

ShowTime Patterns: Big Billy Goat

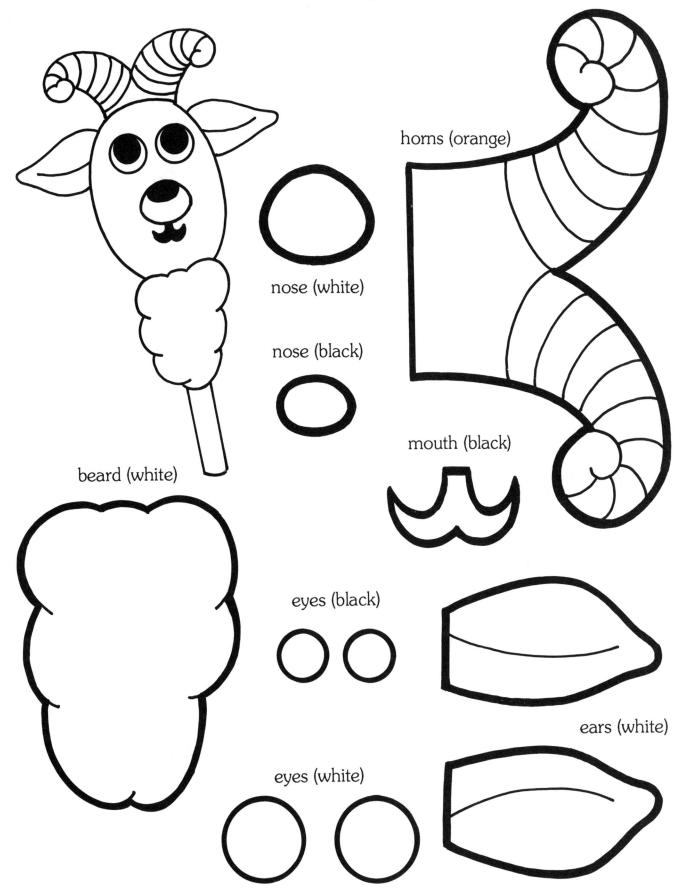

horns (orange)

nose (white)

nose (black)

mouth (black)

beard (white)

eyes (black)

ears (white)

eyes (white)

ShowTime Patterns: Middle-sized Billy Goat

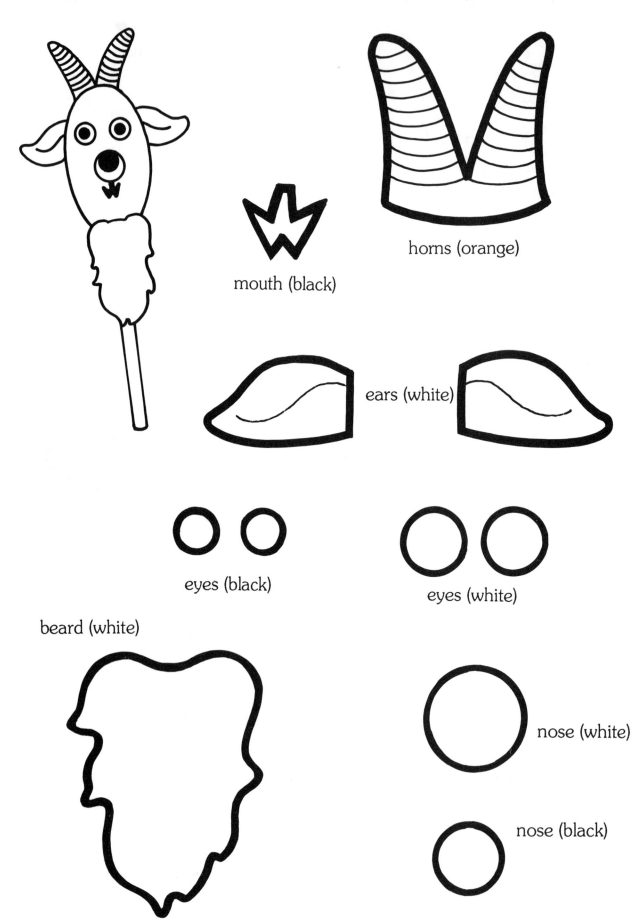

mouth (black)

horns (orange)

ears (white)

eyes (black)

eyes (white)

beard (white)

nose (white)

nose (black)

ShowTime Patterns: Small Billy Goat

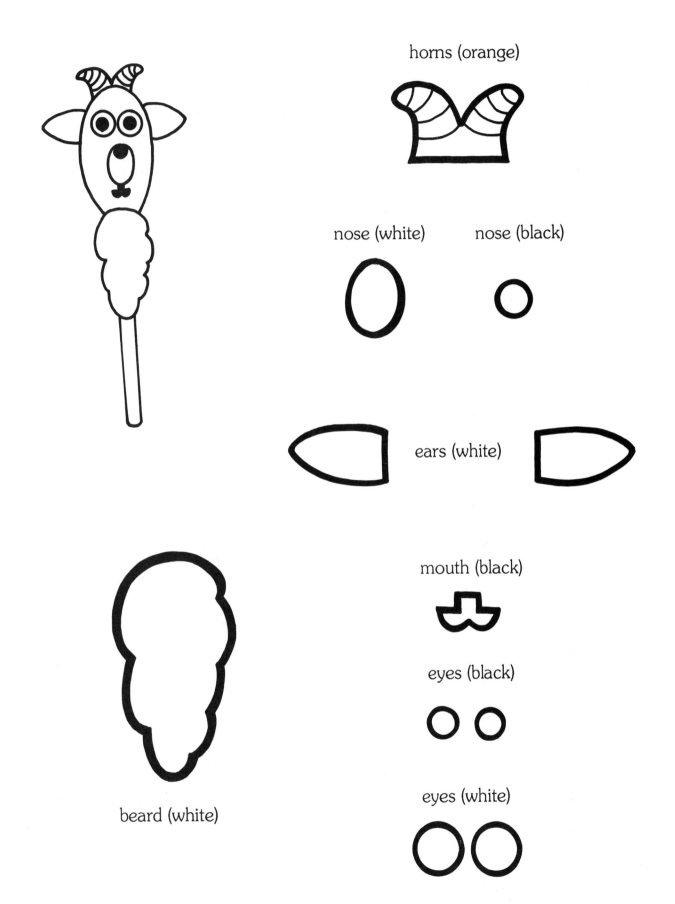

horns (orange)

nose (white)   nose (black)

ears (white)

mouth (black)

eyes (black)

eyes (white)

beard (white)

13

ShowTime Pattern: Bridge

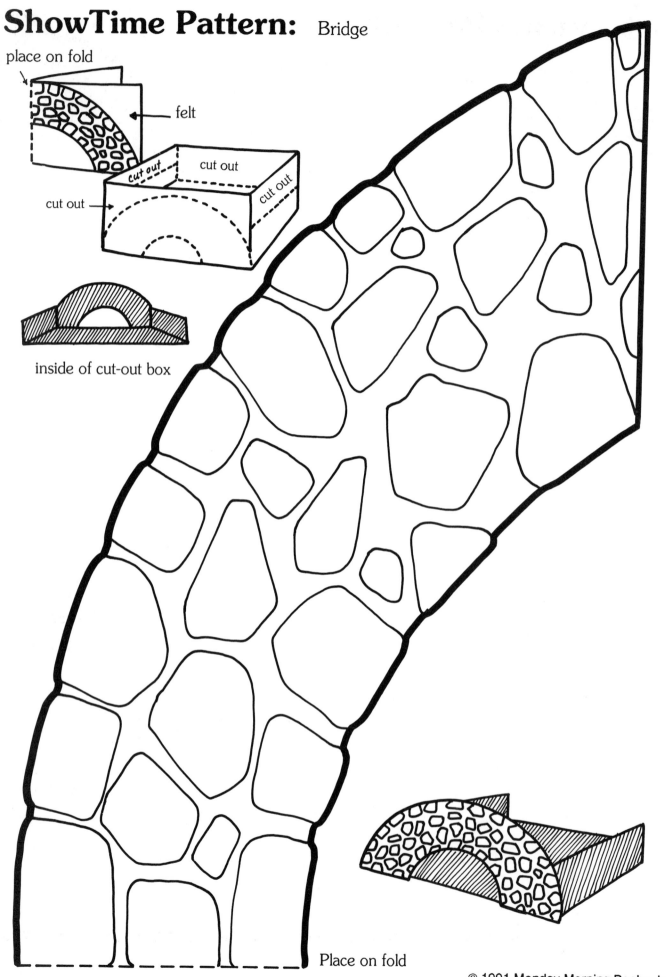

place on fold

felt

cut out

cut out

cut out

cut out

inside of cut-out box

Place on fold

ShowTime Pattern: Grassy Hillside

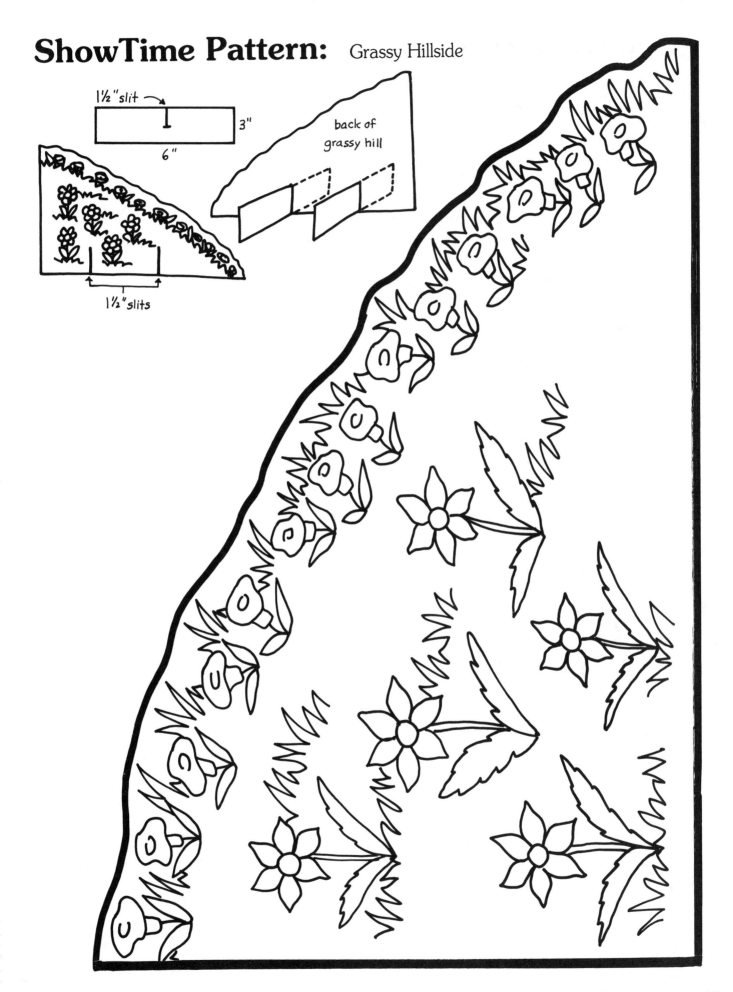

1½" slit

3"

6"

back of grassy hill

1½" slits

Henny Penny

Story Versions

*Henny Penny by Paul Galdone (Clarion, 1968; also published by Scholastic).

When an acorn falls on Henny Penny's head, she thinks the sky is falling and runs to tell the king. Cocky Locky, Ducky Lucky, Goosey Loosey, and Turkey Lurkey all join her. Foxy Loxy tricks them into his cave and they are never seen again. (*This version fits the ShowTime patterns included in this kit.)

Chicken Little by Steven Kellogg (Mulberry, 1985).

In this version, Foxy Loxy disguises himself as a police officer and locks the animals in a poultry truck. Sergeant Hippo Hefty parachutes down and lands on Foxy Loxy. The animals are saved and Foxy Loxy is sent to prison.

The Story of Chicken Licken by Jan Ormerod (Lothrop, Lee & Shepard, 1985).

The story of Chicken Licken is told with illustrations of children performing the story as a stage play.

Also recommended:

Henny Penny by Carol Byer (Troll, 1981).

Henny Penny by Ellen Dolan and Jane Bolinske (Milliken, 1987).

Chicken Little by Karen Schmidt (Putnam, 1986).

Chicken Little by Garvin Bishop (Oxford University Press, 1987).

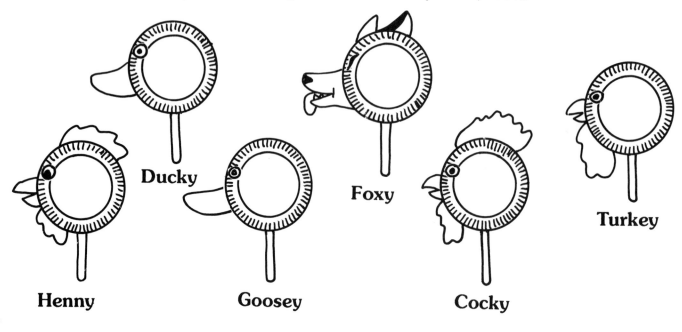

Ducky

Foxy

Turkey

Henny

Goosey

Cocky

LearnTime Chart Activity

Materials: large sheet of butcher paper, marker, at least two versions of
Henny Penny or Chicken Little

Preparation: Make a chart on butcher paper like the one illustrated here.
Hang the chart on a bulletin board or wall.

Activity: Read one version of Henny Penny aloud. Have the children dictate the information to you to fill in the chart. On another day, repeat the process with another version of the story. Compare the versions. Let the children illustrate the chart by drawing and then cutting out pictures to glue onto it.

	Author	Author
Name the characters.		
Who do the characters want to warn?		
What happens to the characters?		
What words do the characters repeat?		

PlayTime Movement Activity

Materials: PlayTime pattern, brown felt, dried beans or rice, scissors, needle and thread, butcher paper, markers

Preparation: Duplicate and cut out enough acorn patterns on the brown felt so there are two for each child. Make acorn-shaped beanbags by placing two patterns together and sewing around the edge, leaving an inch and a half open. Fill the beanbags with beans or rice and sew closed. Next, trace the outline of a child's body onto butcher paper. Use markers to add details to the outline.

Activities: Display the tracing so everyone can see it. Then call out a body part and have each child touch the part with an acorn beanbag. Children can also put their beanbag on their head and try to keep it there as they walk, tiptoe, take big and small steps, or march to fast and slow music. Finally, you can place the body outline on the floor, call out the name of a body part, and have the children toss their beanbags onto the correct part.

ShowTime Play

Characters: Henny Penny, Ducky Lucky, Cocky Locky, Goosey Loosey, Turkey Lurkey, Foxy Loxy

Materials: ShowTime patterns; 6 paper plates; 6 paint stirrers or tongue depressors; yellow, red, white, and black construction paper; green, black, white, red, orange, and brown tempera paint; brushes; scissors; glue; tape or stapler; a cork; a sheet; a chair

Preparation: Cut a hole approximately $5\frac{1}{2}$" in diameter in the center of each paper plate. Paint the paper plates: white with black stripes for Henny Penny; green for Ducky Lucky; orange for Cocky Locky; white for Goosey Loosey; brown for Turkey Lurkey; and red for Foxy Loxy. Duplicate the patterns on the colors of construction paper indicated. Cut out and glue the large patterns to the back of the plates as shown. (See the completed masks on the first page of this kit.) Glue the eyes to the front of the plates. Staple or tape a tongue depressor or paint stirrer to the bottom of each animal mask for a handle.

Activity: Set the stage for the show by placing a sheet-draped chair to one side. Select the children to play the characters and hand out the animal masks. Read or tell the story while the children act out the parts. Begin the show by tossing the cork lightly in the air so it falls on Henny Penny. End the story by having Foxy Loxy lead the other characters into his cave (under the sheet). Let the children say the repetitive dialogue. Repeat the story and action enough times so that every child has the chance to participate.

PlayTime Pattern: Acorn

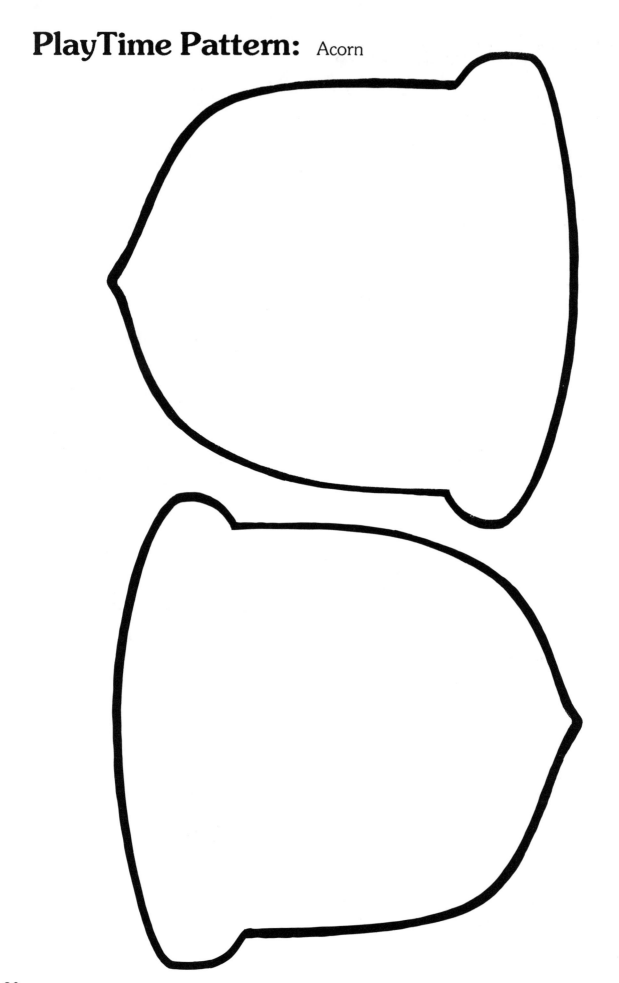

ShowTime Patterns

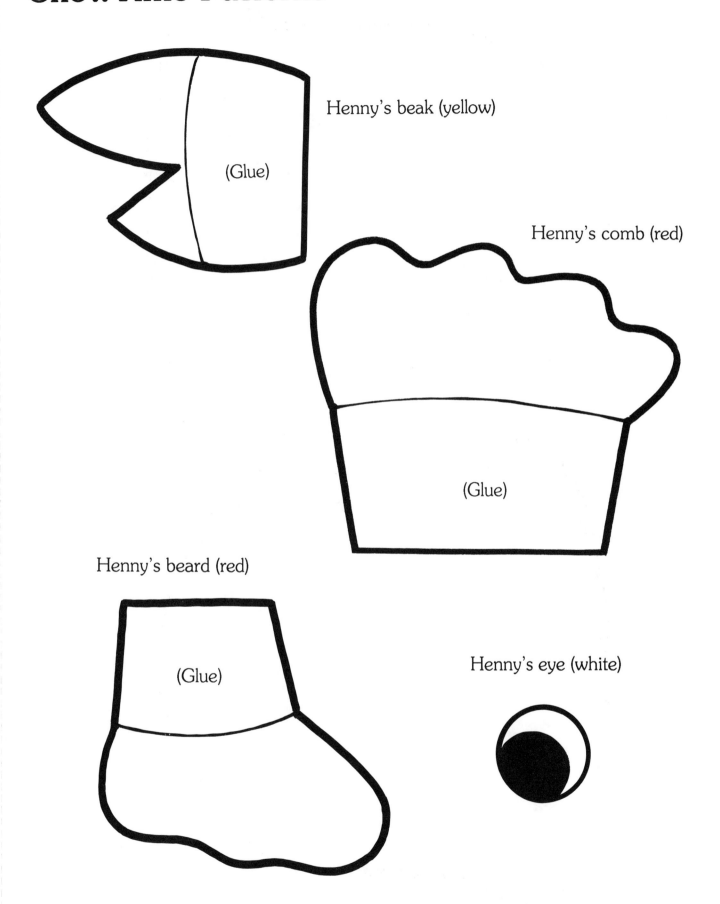

Henny's beak (yellow)

(Glue)

Henny's comb (red)

(Glue)

Henny's beard (red)

(Glue)

Henny's eye (white)

21

ShowTime Patterns

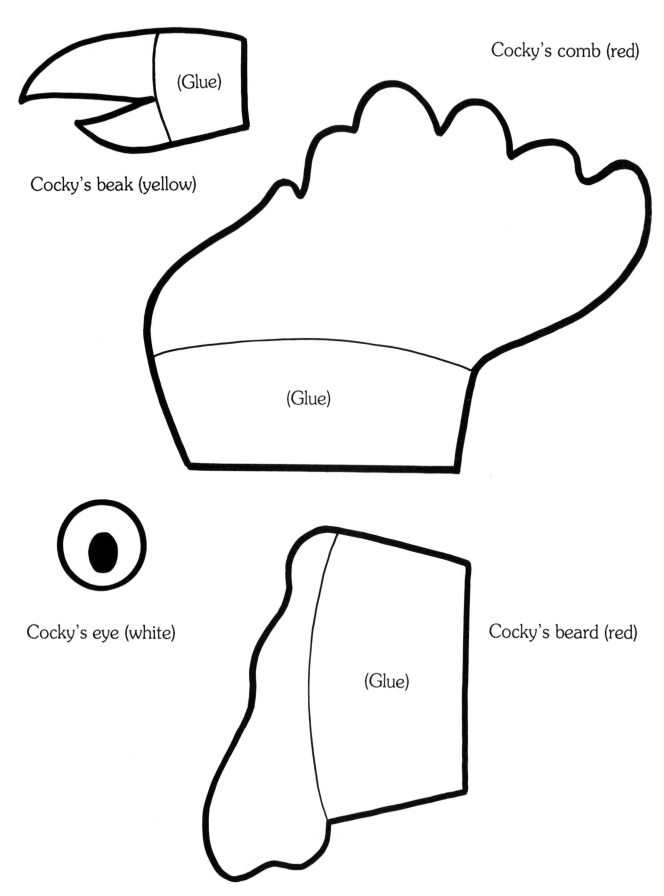

(Glue)

Cocky's beak (yellow)

Cocky's comb (red)

(Glue)

Cocky's eye (white)

(Glue)

Cocky's beard (red)

ShowTime Patterns

Foxy's eye (black)

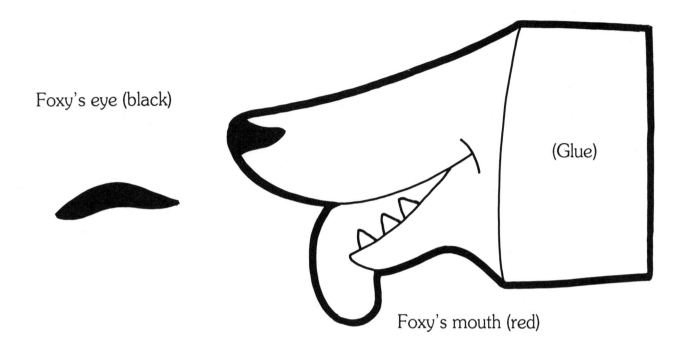

(Glue)

Foxy's mouth (red)

Foxy's ears (red)

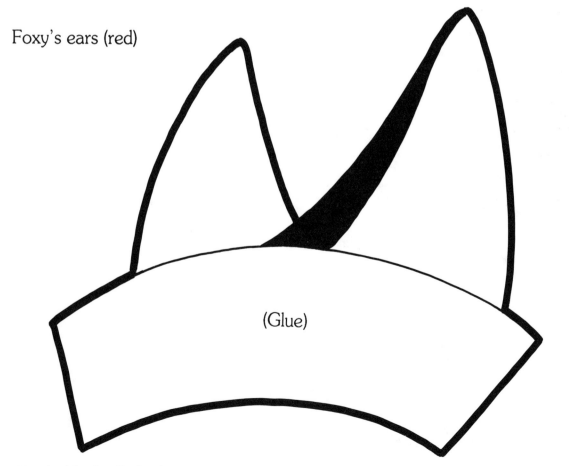

(Glue)

ShowTime Patterns

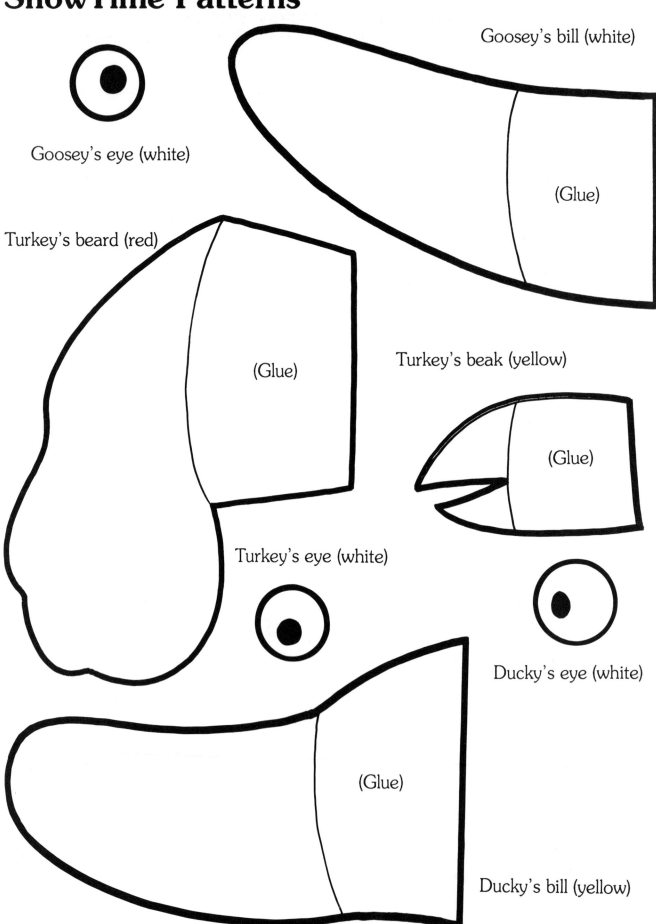

Goosey's eye (white)

Goosey's bill (white)

(Glue)

Turkey's beard (red)

(Glue)

Turkey's beak (yellow)

(Glue)

Turkey's eye (white)

Ducky's eye (white)

(Glue)

Ducky's bill (yellow)

The Little Red Hen

Story Versions

* <u>The Little Red Hen</u> by Lucinda McQueen (Scholastic, 1985). Available in Big Book format.

A little red hen keeps asking her friends—a cat, a dog, and a goose—to help her plant and grow some wheat. The animals refuse to help her. So the hen grows the wheat, threshes it, grinds it into flour, bakes some bread, and eats the bread herself. (*This version fits the ShowTime patterns included in this kit.)

<u>The Little Red Hen</u> by Paul Galdone (Clarion, 1973).

A cat, a dog, and a mouse refuse to help the little red hen, so she bakes a cake by herself. Then the dog, cat, and mouse become eager helpers.

<u>The Little Red Hen: An Old Story</u> by Margot Zemach (Farrar, Straus and Giroux, 1983).

A goose, a cat, and a pig refuse to help the little red hen. Her chicks help her grow the wheat, bake a loaf of bread, and eat it.

Also recommended:

<u>The Little Red Hen</u> by Lyn Calder (Western, 1988).

<u>The Little Red Hen</u> by Tadasu Izawa and Shigemi Hijkata (Putnam, 1981).

<u>The Little Red Hen</u> by Patricia and Fredrick McKissack (Childrens Press, 1985).

<u>The Little Red Hen</u> by William Stobbs (Oxford University Press, 1987).

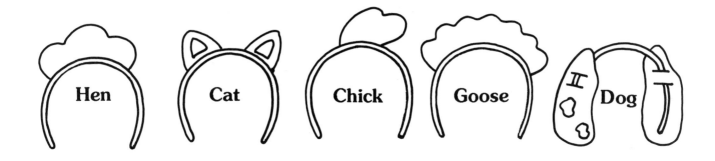

LearnTime Chart Activity

Materials: large sheet of butcher paper, marker, at least two versions of
The Little Red Hen

Preparation: Make a chart on the butcher paper like the one illustrated
here. Hang the chart on a bulletin board or wall.

Activity: Read one version of The Little Red Hen aloud. Have the children
dictate the information to you to complete the chart. On another day, repeat
the process with another version of the story. Compare the two versions. Let
the children illustrate the chart by drawing and then cutting out pictures to
glue onto it.

	Author	Author
Name the characters in the story.		
What does the little red hen do by herself?		
What does the little red hen bake?		
What words does the little red hen repeat?		
What words do the other animals repeat?		

PlayTime Movement Activity

Materials: PlayTime pattern; yellow construction paper; 12 12-inch-long, $\frac{1}{2}$ - inch-diameter dowel sticks; clear Contact paper or laminating film; scissors; masking tape; balance beam (optional)

Preparation: Duplicate the wheat pattern page four times on yellow construction paper to make twelve stalks of wheat. Cut out, or have the children cut out, the pieces. Laminate or cover the wheat with clear Contact paper. Then tape a wheat shape to each dowel stick. Lean the wheat stalks against the balance beam or lay them across a 10-foot line of masking tape on the floor.

Activity: Have the children walk through the wheat field—along the balance beam or tape—harvesting (picking up) the stalks of wheat.

ShowTime Play

Characters: Little Red Hen, Cat, Goose, Dog, Chick (optional)

Materials: ShowTime patterns; white, orange, yellow, brown, black, red, and pink felt; 4 or 5 headbands; glue; ribbon; grains of wheat or seeds; stalks of wheat (real stalks or those from the PlayTime Activity); flour bag stuffed with paper; bread pan; spoon and bowl; scissors; hole punch; table or cardboard box; tablecloth; chairs; glue or hot glue gun; marker; water

Preparation: Duplicate the patterns on the colors of felt indicated and cut them out. Glue two felt spots to each dog's ear. Wet the hen's comb, the cat's ears, the chick's comb (optional), and the goose's headdress with water. Fold them on the dotted lines as indicated on the patterns. Place a book or other heavy object on each folded section and let the patterns dry with the top at a right angle to the bottom (see the illustration). When the patterns are dry, attach each folded portion to a headband with glue. Make two cuts at the top of each dog's ear where indicated and slide the ears onto a headband. Next, trace the feet patterns on the colors of felt indicated and cut them out. Cut through the patterns on the dotted lines. Punch holes where indicated and slide lengths of ribbon through. (See the completed headbands on the first page.)

Activity: Set the stage by arranging a table or cardboard box covered with a tablecloth to one side. Place the bread pan, bowl, and spoon on the table. Create the wheat field area on the other side of the stage by laying the stalks of wheat in front of two or three chairs. Select a child for each character in the story and help the children put on the appropriate animal headbands and feet. Read or tell the story, letting the children act out their parts and add dialogue. After the little red hen plants the wheat (spreads the grains or seeds), have her prop up the stalks of wheat against the chairs. When she harvests the wheat, have her knock the stalks down. When she threshes the wheat, let her pretend to beat the wheat. Have her pick up the empty flour sack when it's time to grind the wheat into flour. Repeat the story and action enough times so that every child has a chance to participate.

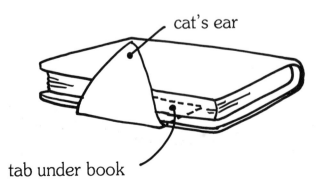

cat's ear

tab under book

28

PlayTime Pattern: Wheat

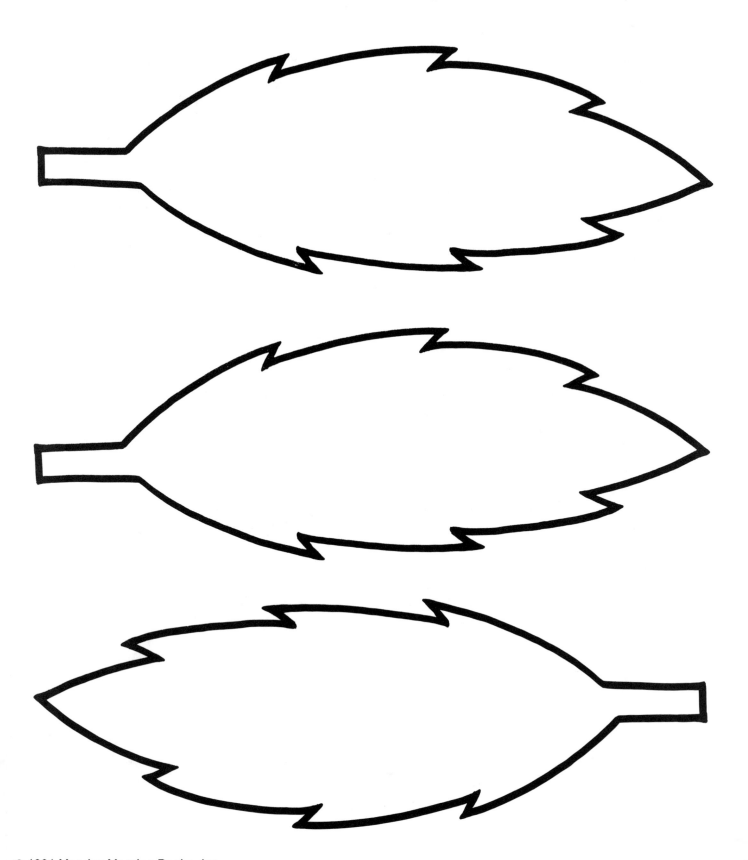

ShowTime Patterns

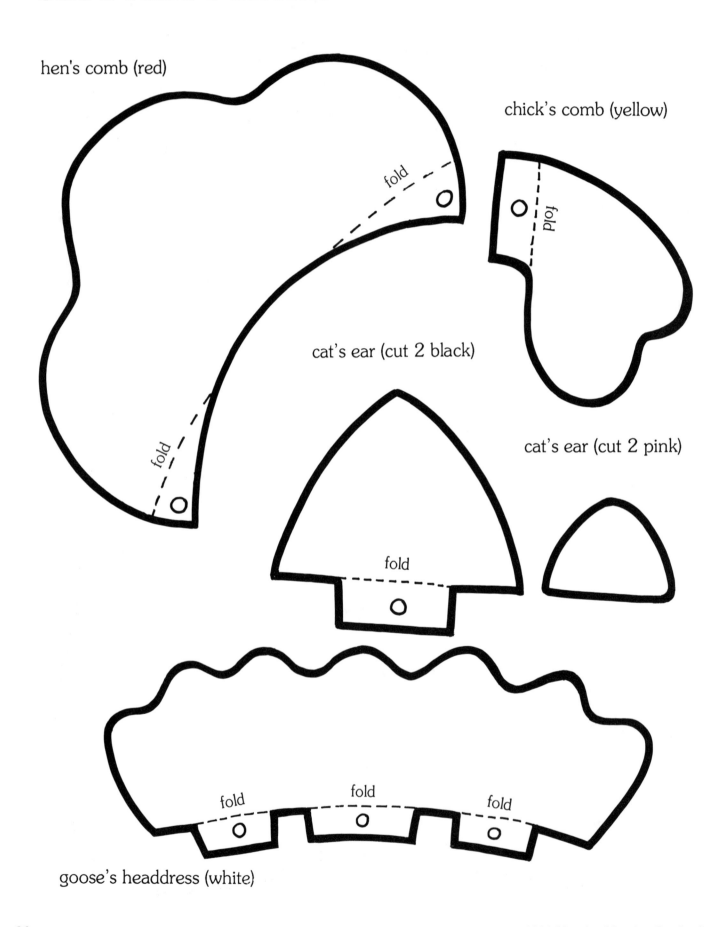

hen's comb (red)

chick's comb (yellow)

fold

fold

fold

cat's ear (cut 2 black)

cat's ear (cut 2 pink)

fold

goose's headdress (white)

fold   fold   fold

ShowTime Patterns

dog's spots (white)

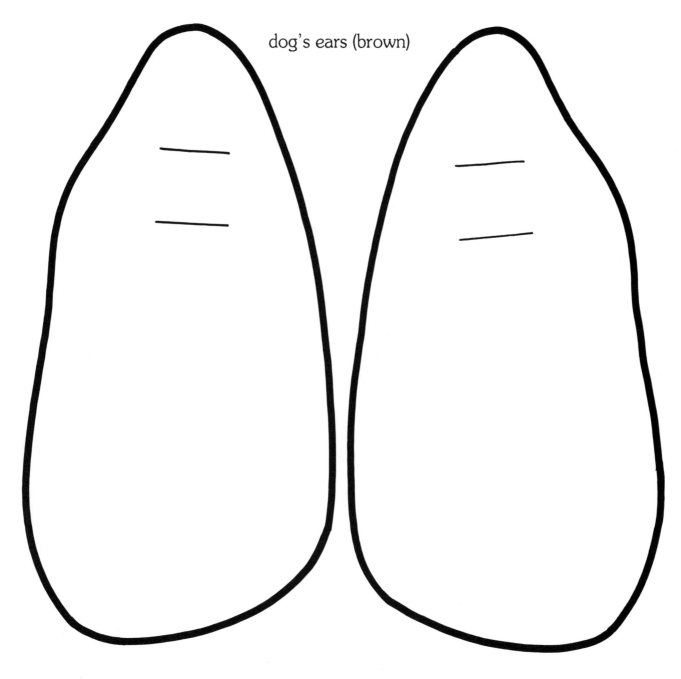

dog's ears (brown)

ShowTime Pattern: Feet

hen (orange)

chick (yellow)

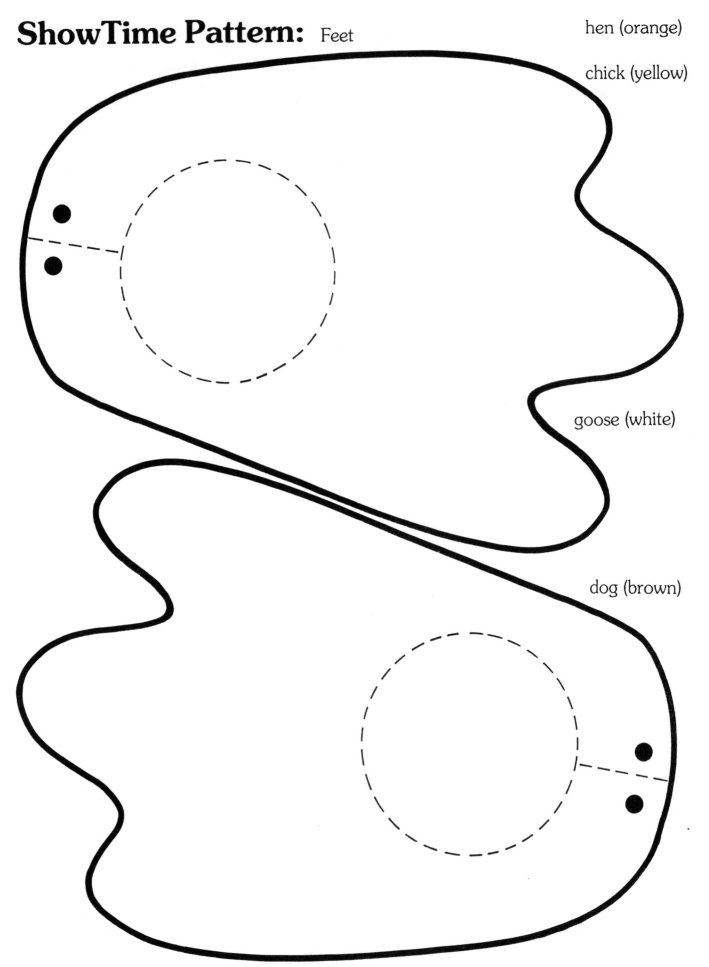

goose (white)

dog (brown)

The Turnip

Story Versions

*The Enormous Turnip by Kathy Parkinson (Albert Whitman & Company, 1986).

Grandfather Ivan grows such an enormous turnip that he can't pull it up. Grandmother, mother, granddaughter, puppy, kitten, and mouse all pull with grandfather but still they can't pull the turnip up. Finally a beetle helps, and out pops the turnip. Everyone eats the turnip for dinner. (*This version fits the ShowTime patterns included in this kit.)

The Turnip by Janina Domanska (Macmillan, 1969).

It takes grandfather, grandmother, grandson, dog, cat, gander, goose, rooster, hen, and pig to pull out the turnip.

The Great Big Enormous Turnip by Helen Oxenbury (Franklin Watts, 1968).

An old man, old woman, granddaughter, dog, cat, and mouse pull up the turnip.

Also recommended:

Tale of the Great Big Enormous Turnip by Anita Hewett (Whittlessy House, 1961).

The Turnip by Pier Morgan (Philomel, 1990).

The Turnip by Alexei Tolstoi (Malysh Publishers, undated).

Dog   **Mouse**   **Granddaughter**   **Mother**   **Grandfather**

LearnTime Chart Activity

Materials: large sheet of butcher paper, marker, at least two versions of The Turnip

Preparation: Make a chart on the butcher paper like the one illustrated here. Hang the chart on a bulletin board or wall.

Activity: Read one version of The Turnip aloud. Have the children dictate the information to you to fill in the chart. On another day, repeat the process with another version of the story. Compare the versions. Let the children illustrate the chart by drawing and then cutting out pictures to glue onto it.

	Author	Author
Name the characters.		
Who is the first character to try to pull up the turnip?		
Who is the last character to help pull up the turnip?		
What words are repeated in the story?		

PlayTime Movement Activity

Activity: Have the children hold hands in a circle and move around the circle as they sing the following song:

(To the tune of "Ring Around the Rosie")

Ring around the garden,

Pockets full of turnips,

Pull-ll, pull-ll,

All fall down!

At the words "Pull-ll, pull-ll," tell the children to act as if they are pulling a big, stubborn turnip out of the ground. Then let them act as if the turnip pops out, and have everyone fall down.

ShowTime Play

Characters: Grandfather, Grandmother, Mother, Granddaughter, Dog, Cat, Mouse, Beetle

Materials: ShowTime patterns; 12" x 18" sheets of black, orange, purple, gray, blue, pink, yellow, and red construction paper or felt; smaller pieces of white, red, black, gray, blue, and pink construction paper or felt; a large turnip; buttons; lace; ribbon; fabric; scissors; glue; 2 black pipe cleaners; stapler; black marker

Preparation: Fold the 12" x 18" pieces of construction paper or felt in half so each forms a 12" x 9" shape. Place each collar pattern on the fold of the appropriate color of paper or felt as indicated. Trace and cut out the patterns. Duplicate and cut out the smaller patterns and details as indicated. Color in the black parts of the eyes. Glue the small pieces to the appropriate collars as indicated. If you wish, add lace, fabric, ribbon, and buttons to the collars for more detail. Staple the two pipe cleaners to the beetle collar for antennae. Staple a round antenna pattern to the end of each pipe cleaner. Cut all the way up the center of the back of each completed collar so the children can put the collars on easily.

Activity: Set the stage by placing the turnip on the floor to one side. If you want to end the story with all the characters pretending to eat the turnip, add a table with bowls and spoons to the stage. Select a child to play each character. Have those children put on the appropriate collar. Then read or tell the story while the children act out the parts and add dialogue. Repeat the story enough times so that every child has a chance to participate.

Grandmother

Beetle

Cat

cut

ShowTime Pattern: Collar—Granddaughter (red), Cat (orange)

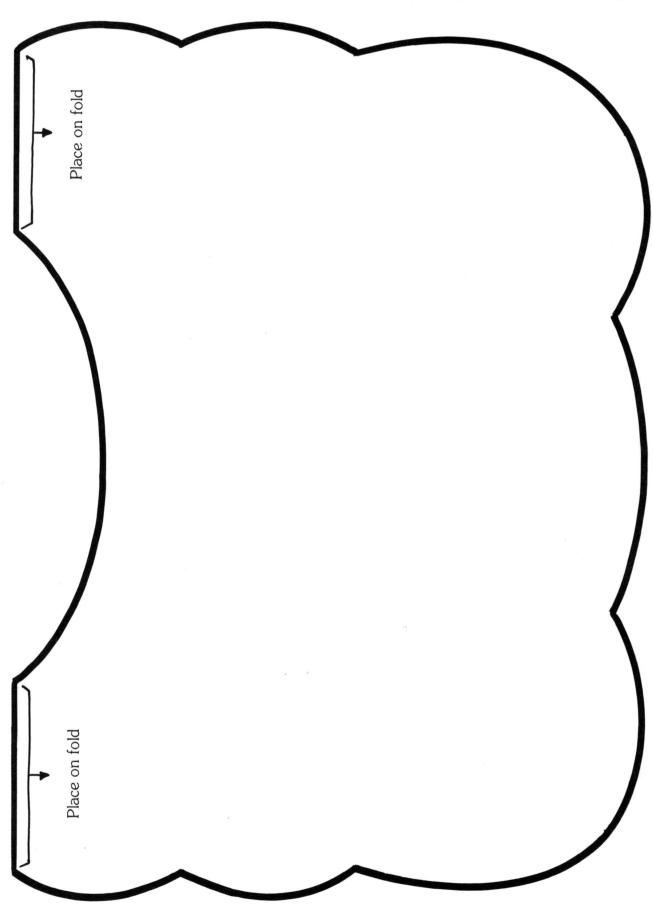

Place on fold

Place on fold

ShowTime Pattern: Collar—Mouse (pink)

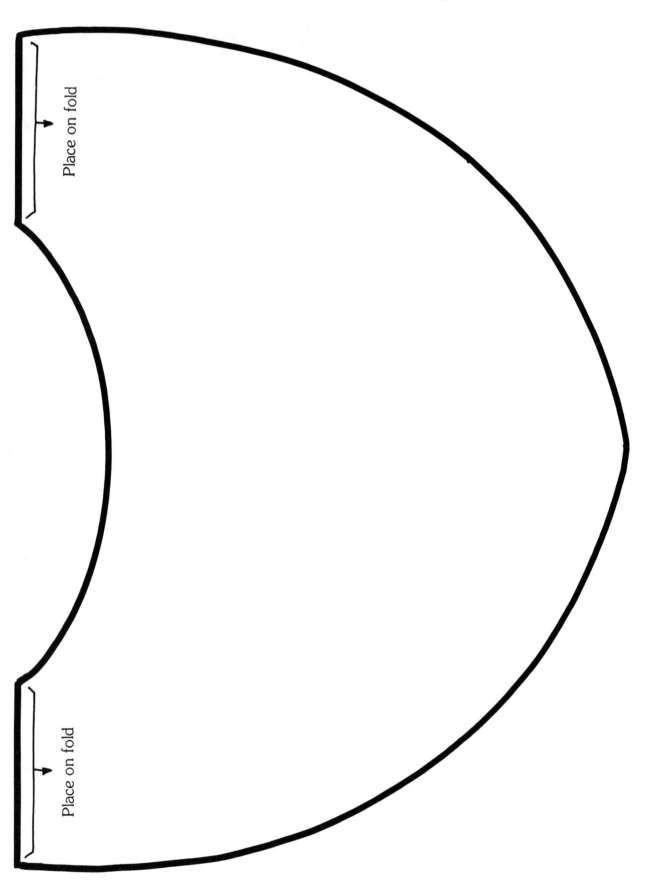

Place on fold

Place on fold

ShowTime Pattern: Collar—Beetle (black)

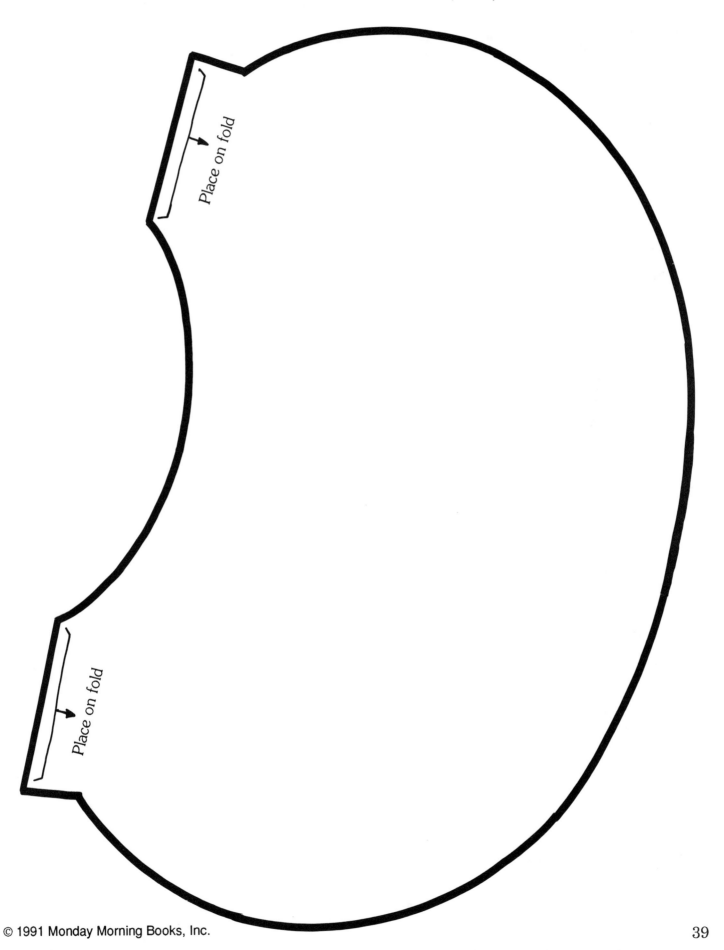

Place on fold

Place on fold

ShowTime Pattern: Collar—Grandfather (blue),
Mother (yellow), Dog (gray)

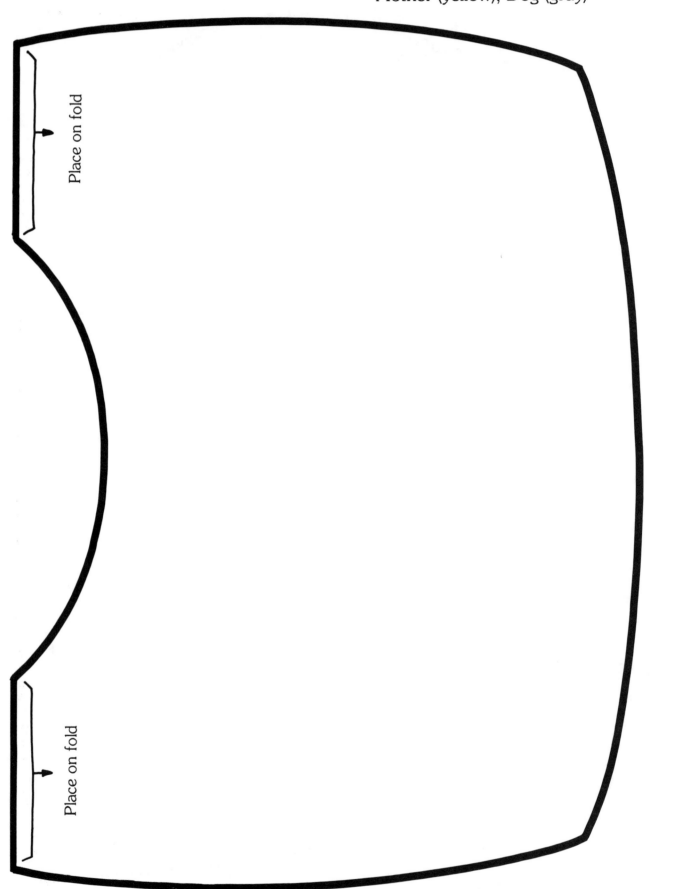

Place on fold

Place on fold

ShowTime Pattern: Collar—Grandmother (purple)

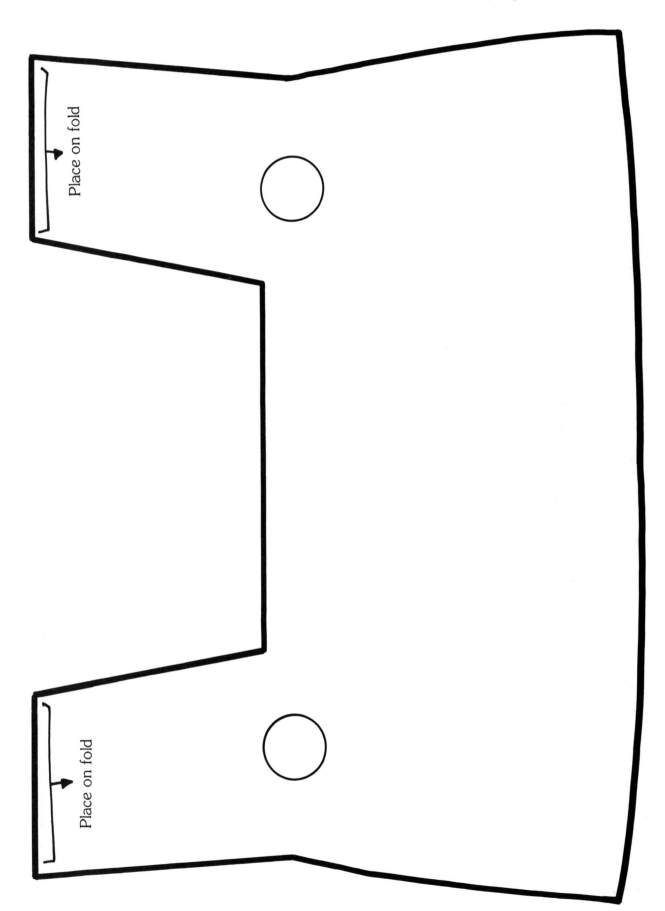

Place on fold

Place on fold

ShowTime Patterns

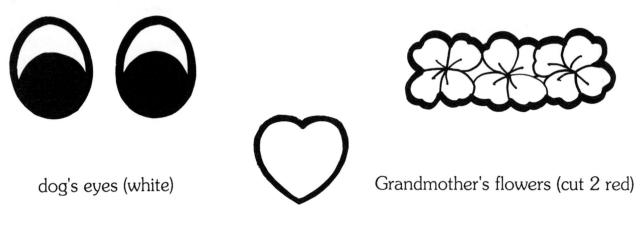

dog's eyes (white)

Grandmother's flowers (cut 2 red)

Grandmother's heart (red)

dog's ear (black)

dog's nose
(pink)

dog's ear (black)

ShowTime Patterns

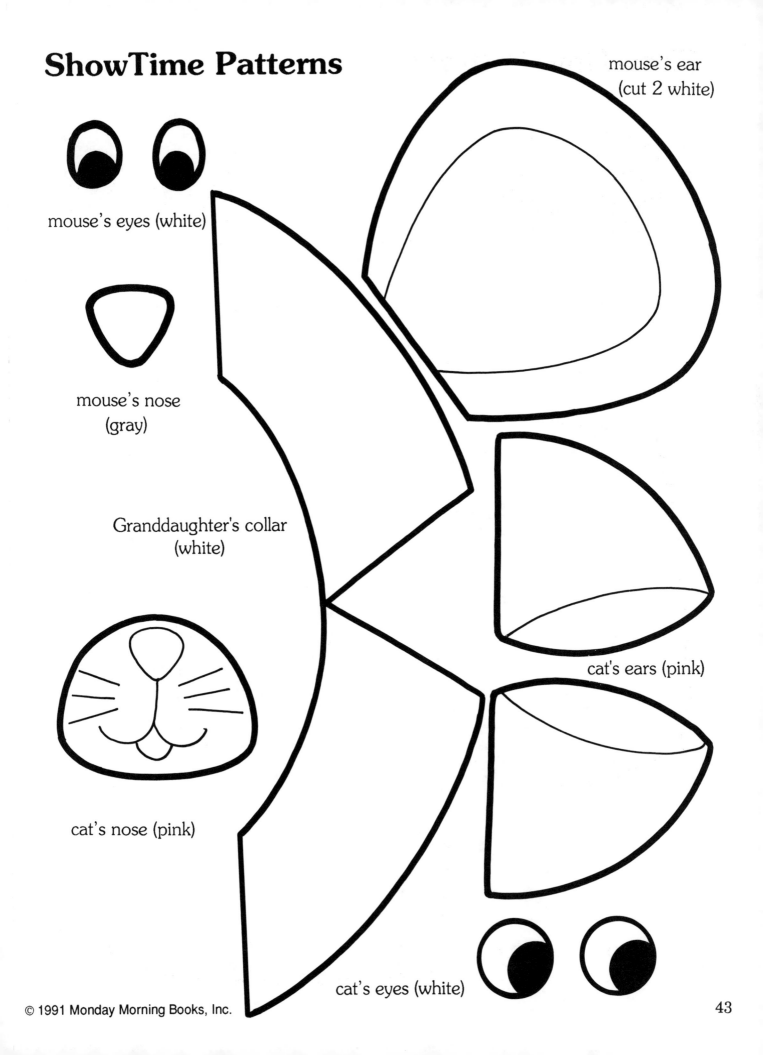

mouse's ear
(cut 2 white)

mouse's eyes (white)

mouse's nose
(gray)

Granddaughter's collar
(white)

cat's ears (pink)

cat's nose (pink)

cat's eyes (white)

ShowTime Patterns

beetle's eyes (white)

mother's necklace (red)

beetle's antenna (cut 2 black)

Grandfather's shirt front (white)

Grandfather's pocket

44

The Three Little Pigs

Story Versions

*The Three Little Pigs by Paul Galdone (Clarion, 1970).

Three little pigs leave their mother to seek their fortunes. One pig builds a house with straw, one with sticks, and one with bricks. A wolf destroys the first two houses but can't blow down the house made of bricks. The wolf tries to entice the pig out of the brick house to pick turnips, pick apples, and go to a fair. But the little pig ends up cooking the wolf for supper. (*This version fits the ShowTime patterns included in this kit.)

The Three Little Pigs by Gavin Bishop (Scholastic, 1989).

In this version the three pigs lounge around a pool, their mom has a perm and wears thongs, and the wolf wears shades and carries a portable tape player. Despite these modern touches, the tale ends in the traditional way.

The Three Little Pigs by Edda Reinl (Picture Book Studio, 1983).

The first two pigs don't get eaten in this version—they run to the safety of the third pig's house. The wolf isn't eaten either; he gets so angry he bursts like a giant balloon.

The True Story of the Three Little Pigs by Jon Scieszka (Viking Kestrel, 1989).

This version is told from the wolf's perspective. He claims he's been framed— he only blew down the houses because he sneezed accidentally.

Also recommended:

The Three Little Pigs by Aurelius Battaglia (Random House, 1977).

The Three Little Pigs by Erik Belgvad (Atheneum, 1984).

The Story of the Three Little Pigs by Lorinda Cauley (Putnam, 1980).

The Three Little Pigs and the Fox by William Hooks (Macmillan, 1989).

The Three Little Pigs by James Marshall (Dial, 1989).

The Three Little Pigs by Margot Zemach (Farrar, Straus and Giroux, 1988).

LearnTime Chart Activity

Materials: large sheet of butcher paper, marker, at least two versions of The Three Little Pigs

Preparation: Make a chart on the butcher paper like the one illustrated here. Hang the chart on a bulletin board or wall.

Activity: Read one version of The Three Little Pigs aloud. Have the children dictate the information to you to fill in the chart. On another day, repeat the process with another version. Compare the two versions. Let the children illustrate the chart by drawing and then cutting out pictures to glue onto it.

	Author	Author
What happens to the first two little pigs?		
What happens to the wolf?		
What words do the pigs repeat?		
What do the characters look like? the pigs		
the wolf		

PlayTime Movement Activity

Materials: PlayTime pattern, black poster board, 18" x 18" x 12" cardboard box, $\frac{1}{2}$-yard fake fur, dried beans or rice, needle and thread, tape, scissors, marker

Preparation: Cut out the stew pot pattern. Trace the pattern on black poster board, then turn the pattern over and trace it again to make one complete pot. Trace a second complete pot. Cut the pots out and tape one to the front and one to the back of the box. Cut the fake fur into several five-inch squares. Make "wolf" beanbags from the squares by sewing two squares together around the edges, leaving a one-and-a-half-inch opening. Fill the squares with beans or rice and sew up the opening.

Activity: Have the children take turns tossing the wolf (a beanbag) into the stew pot (the box).

ShowTime Puppet Show

Characters: Three Little Pigs, Mother Pig, Wolf

Materials: ShowTime patterns; tagboard or poster board; small sticks, twigs, or toothpicks; bits of straw or hay; 4 clean half-gallon plastic milk containers; 2 cardboard tubes; brown tempera paint; brush; green and red construction paper; markers; clear Contact paper or laminating film; scissors; craft knife; glue; 5 tongue depressors; stapler; large table

Preparation: Duplicate the character patterns on tagboard or poster board. Cut out the patterns and color them with markers as indicated. Laminate or cover the patterns with clear Contact paper. Glue a tongue depressor to the back of each character for a handle. Next, duplicate the stick and straw house pattern twice on tagboard. Duplicate the brick house pattern and the fair tent pattern once each on tagboard. Cut the patterns out; cut out the window openings. Color the houses and the tent with markers. Glue sticks or twigs to one house and hay or straw to the other. To make stands for the houses and tent, cut the top and one side off each milk container as shown. Glue a house or tent to each container. Cut house windows in the containers.

cut

To make two apple trees, cut a cardboard tube into two six-inch sections. Paint with brown tempera. Duplicate and cut out two treetop patterns from green construction paper and ten to twelve apples from red construction paper. Color the apple leaves green, then glue the apples to the treetops. Laminate or cover the treetops with clear Contact paper. Staple a treetop to each painted tube. To make the turnip patch, duplicate the pattern on tagboard or poster board. Color with markers. Make a stand for the pattern by cutting the other cardboard tube into two pieces and stapling them to the back of the pattern.

Activity: Set the stage by placing the three houses on one side of the large table. Place the apple trees, the turnip patch, and the tent on the other side of the table. Select a child for each character in the story and distribute the puppets. Have the children use the puppets to act out their parts as you read or retell the tale. Let the children hide their puppets in the houses and knock over the houses at the appropriate times. Repeat the performance enough times so that every child has the chance to participate.

PlayTime Pattern: Stew Pot

ShowTime Patterns: Little Pigs (pink), Mother Pig (pink with blue apron), Wolf (brown)

ShowTime Pattern: Straw House and Stick House (cut 2)

ShowTime Pattern: Brick House

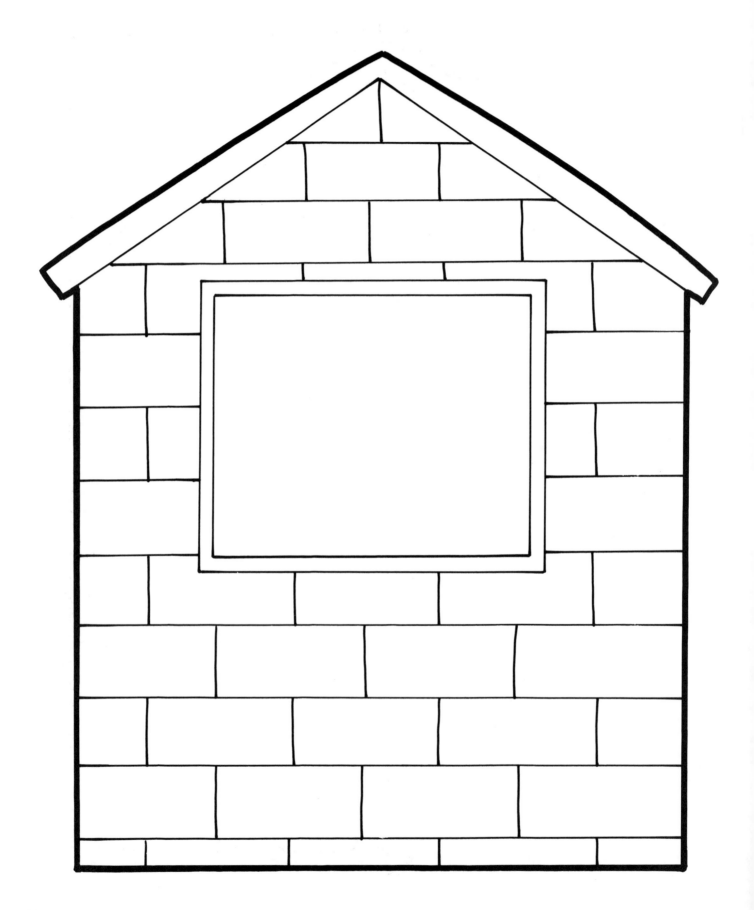

ShowTime Pattern: Fair Tent

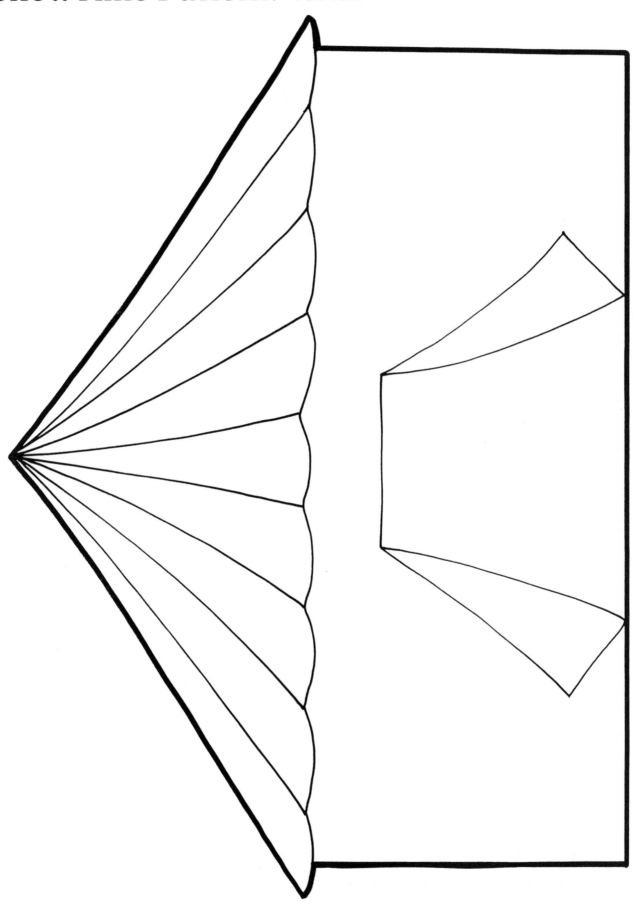

ShowTime Patterns

apple treetop
(green)

apples (red)

turnip patch (green leaves, purple roots)

fence (brown)

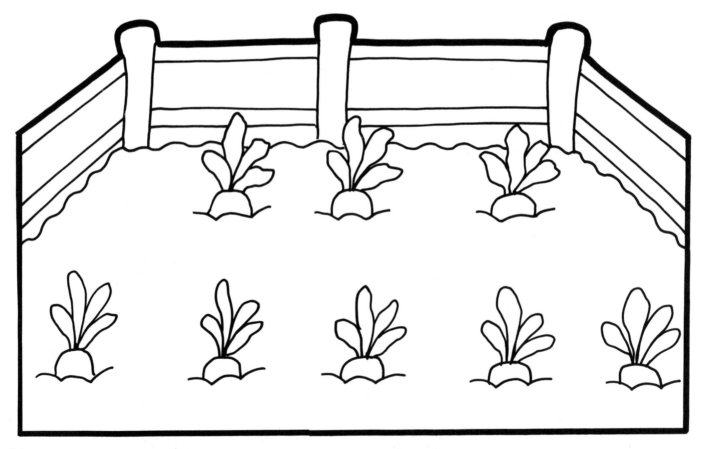

54

The Three Bears

Story Versions

*The Three Bears by Paul Galdone (Clarion, 1972).

One morning while three bears—a wee bear, a middle-sized bear, and a great big bear—are out walking in the woods, a little girl named Goldilocks comes to their house. Goldilocks tries the three bears' porridge, chairs, and beds. When the three bears return home, they find Goldilocks and frighten her away. (*This version fits the ShowTime patterns included with this kit.)

Goldilocks and the Three Bears by Jan Brett (Dodd, Mead & Company, 1987).

Goldilocks is illustrated as a spoiled, willful child. The story ends with a chastened Goldilocks cuddled in her mother's arms; she makes up her mind to never again make herself so much at home in other people's houses.

Goldilocks and the Three Bears by Janet Stevens (Holiday House, 1986).

This version of the story takes place in a modern-day country home.

Also recommended:

Deep in the Forest by Brinton Turkle (Dutton, 1976).

Goldilocks and the Three Bears by James Marshall (Dial, 1988).

The Three Bears by Robin Spouart (Knopf, 1987).

The Story of the Three Bears by William Stobbs (McGraw-Hill, 1965).

Goldilocks and the Three Bears by Bernadette Watts (North-South, 1984).

LearnTime Chart Activity

Materials: large sheet of butcher paper, marker, at least two versions of The Three Bears

Preparation: Make a chart on the butcher paper like the one illustrated here. Hang the chart on a bulletin board or wall.

Activity: Read one version of The Three Bears aloud. Have the children dictate information to you to fill in the chart. On another day, repeat the process with another version of the story. Compare the versions. Let the children illustrate the chart by drawing and then cutting out pictures to glue onto it.

	Author	Author
How are the three bears dressed?		
What sets of 3 are included in the story?		
Why didn't Goldilocks like the large and medium-sized beds?		
What words are repeated by the bears?		

PlayTime Movement Activity

Materials: PlayTime pattern, brown construction paper, clear Contact paper or laminating film, scissors

Preparation: Duplicate the bear print pattern 30 times on brown construction paper. Cut the prints out and laminate or cover them with clear Contact paper. Place the prints on the floor to make a trail around the room.

Activity: Have the students track bears by stepping on, over, between, and beside the bear prints. Then let the children jump over, tiptoe around, and stomp on the prints.

ShowTime Play

Characters: Goldilocks, Mama Bear, Papa Bear, Baby Bear

Materials: ShowTime patterns; 4 pieces of poster board; decorating materials such as fabric, lace, buttons, and ribbon remnants (optional); stapler; markers; 1 yard of 1"-wide ribbon; glue; brown construction paper; 1 large, 1 medium-sized, and 1 small chair; 1 large, 1 medium-sized, and 1 small bowl; 3 spoons; small table or large cardboard box and tablecloth; 3 pieces of fabric approximately 50" x 42", 40" x 32", and 30" x 22"; scissors; craft knife

Preparation: Begin by making the headbands. Duplicate three ear band and three back band patterns on brown construction paper and cut them out. Color the ear details with a black marker. Staple a back band to each ear band so the completed headbands fit the children's heads. To make the costumes, cut each poster board into two 14" x 18" pieces. Enlarge the costume patterns to fit the poster board pieces. Duplicate each of the patterns twice on poster board and cut them out. Color each pattern with markers or add decorating materials to form a front and back piece for each costume. Staple a length of wide ribbon to the front and back of each costume at the shoulder. See the completed costumes on the first page of this kit.

Activity: Set the stage by arranging the three chairs in the center. To one side, place the small table or large cardboard box and tablecloth. Put the spoons and bowls on the table. On the other side of the stage, lay the three pieces of fabric—the beds—on the floor.

Select a child to play each character. Help the children put on their costumes by tying the front and back pieces together at the shoulders. Then read or tell the story as the children act out their parts. Let the children say the repetitive dialogue. Repeat the performance enough times so that every child has the chance to participate.

PlayTime Pattern: Bear Paw Print

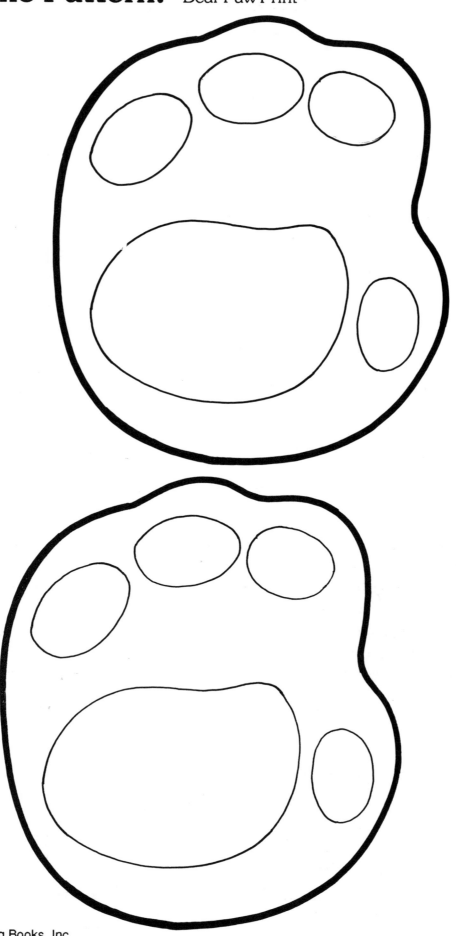

ShowTime Pattern: Bear Headband

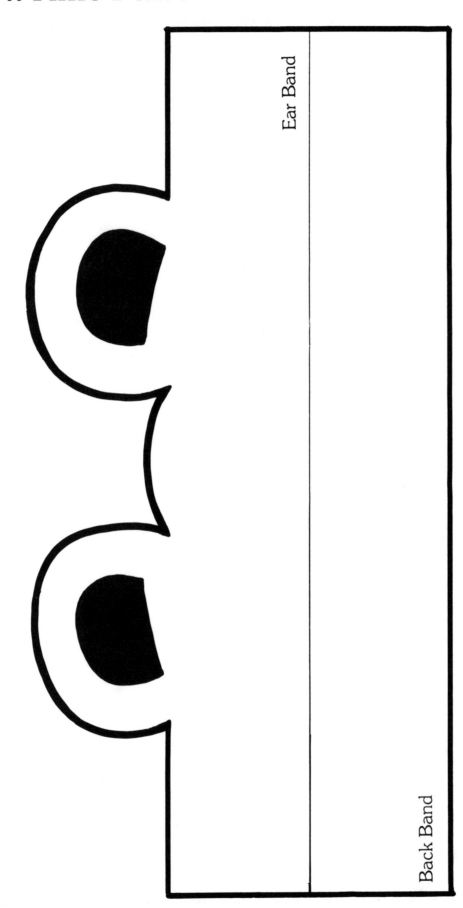

Ear Band

Back Band

ShowTime Pattern: Papa Bear

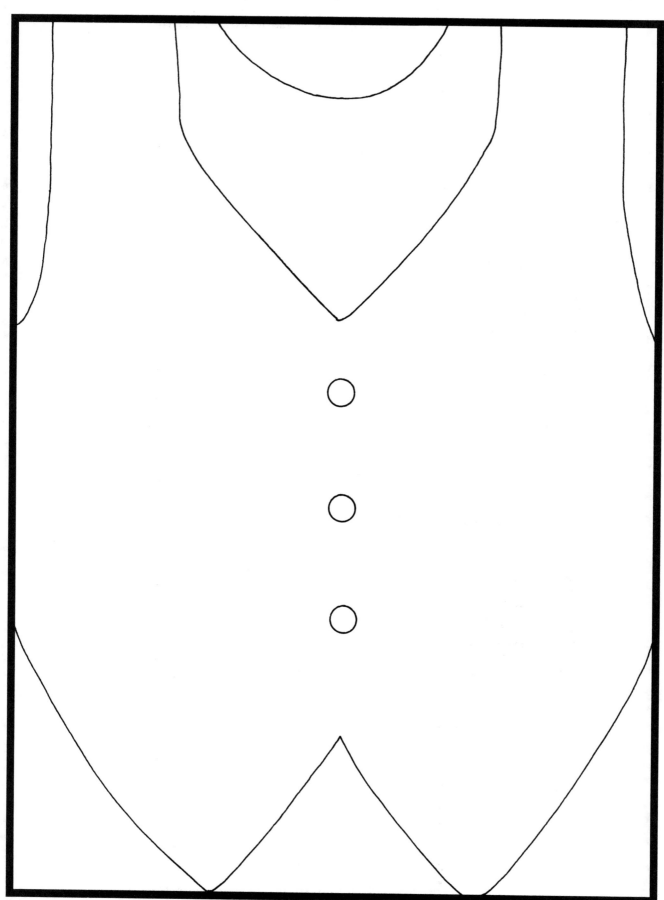

ShowTime Pattern: Mama Bear

Home
Sweet
Home

ShowTime Pattern: Baby Bear

B. B.

ShowTime Pattern: Goldilocks

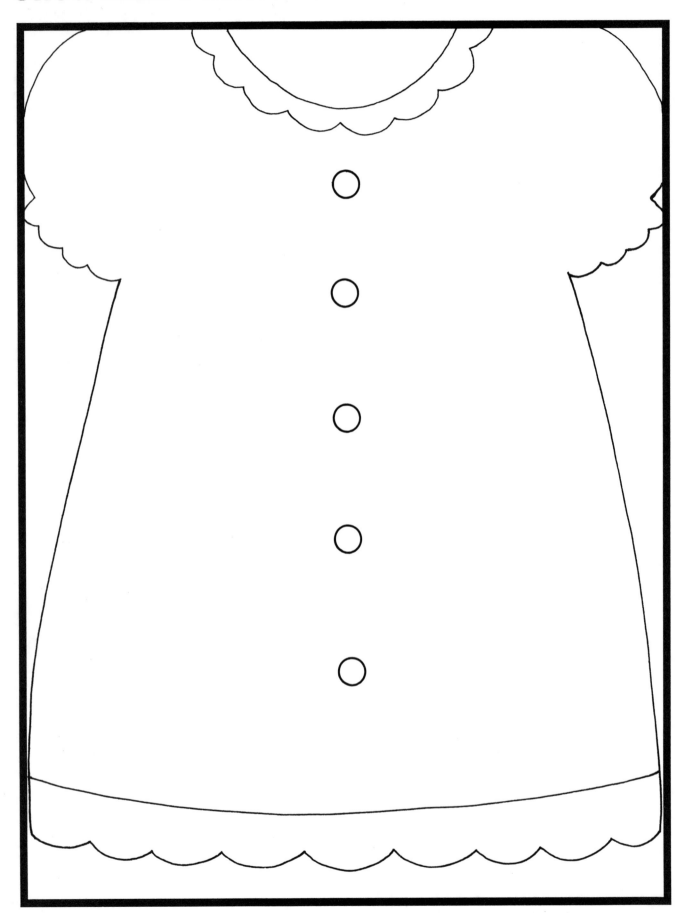